The Basic Guide to US Tariffs

2nd Edition 2025

By Reginald D. Smith

I0502661

Cover Art: Cargo ships with shipping containers. From
the National Oceanic and Atmospheric Administration
(NOAA).

First Printing, 2019

Second Edition, 2025

ISBN: 9781097507801

Supreme Vinegar LLC
PO Box 705
Bensalem, PA 19020

Table of Contents

Introduction

This book came out of efforts to communicate basic ideas about tariffs and their handling in the context of supply chain management. While tariffs never went away, the sheer impact and pervasiveness of them in the current US economy has caught many off guard and let to many requests for information on how to forecast, manage, and negotiate tariff related price increases.

Much information was gained by the author after over 11 years of practical experience working in the Global Supply Chain group of a segment of the ITT Corporation. The author is indebted to many co-workers, especially in the Trade Compliance group, for information and tactics on dealing with foreign trade.

In addition, there is much practical information online. Of course the basic sites to consult are the Customs and Border Patrol (cbp.gov), the US International Trade Commision (usitc.gov) and the Office of the Trade Representative (ustr.gov). In addition, however, are many blogs that often discuss trade law in various detail and give many practice tips. Some of the better ones are the blog of Neville Peterson LLP (www.npllptradelaw.com/blog/) and Crowell Moring (https://www.cmtradelaw.com/). The author has not used these firms and does not endorse them though they provide helpful information.

This book's purpose is to be a basic introduction in understanding the tariff regime and dealing with it. This is not a detailed how-to on import/export or customs brokerage. This is a very detailed process covered in much larger and more comprehensive books and requires years of experience. It also leaves out certain aspects such as determining country of origin for a good. This process is also extremely detailed and will not be covered here where country of origin will be seen as given. Primarily this is an educational guide and can only be as up to date as its most recent printing. Information that is consistent over time, rather than minutiae, are its primary focus.

The second edition updates changes that reflect the new tariffs of the Trump administration as well as trade preference groups such as the African Growth and Opportunity Act and other tariff groups in Chapters 98 and 99.

Dealing with tariffs is not impossible though not always straightforward. This book assumes no prior knowledge and will help everyone from a small business to someone changing roles in a larger company understand the basics and know where to go in seeking more information or professional assistance.

Reginald Smith
February 2025

Chapter 1
A brief history of American tariffs

The struggle between free trade and protecting local industries is as old as civilization. Since central governments emerged many have tried to balance or control trade with others according to elite interests, national interests, war, or popular opinion. In the American case, trade issues go back not only to the beginning of the Republic but its first struggles with Great Britain over trade issues.

After the Revolution, trade again became an issue with our first written constitution, the Articles of Confederation. The Articles envisioned a weak central government and allowed the states to impose tariffs on goods from each other. This caused disputes and economic fragmentation in the new country. After drafting and approving the US Constitution, the internal situation was resolved by Article 1, Section 9.

No tax or duty shall be laid on articles exported from any state.

No preference shall be given by any regulation of commerce or revenue to the ports of one state over those of another: nor shall vessels bound to, or from, one state, be obliged to enter, clear or pay duties in another.

However, though the federal government had powers to implement external tariffs per Article I, Section 8 ("To regulate commerce with foreign nations"), tariffs were controversial and would remain so for decades.

Alexander Hamilton, the first Treasury Secretary, wanted tariffs to protect the nascent industries from cheap European imports. Since these factories were mostly in the North, they aided Northern industrialists while raising prices of manufactured goods for consumers, some of the largest of which were in the plantation driven Southern states. Various compromises were proposed, most notably the American System of Senator Henry Clay of Kentucky that proposed using tariff revenues to fund infrastructure and development in the South and new Midwestern states.

Many debates on the tariff, most famously the Webster-Hayne debates, roiled the Senate before the Civil War "The United States Senate, A.D. 1850." Robert Whitechurch, after Peter Frederick Rothermel (1855)

Eventually tariffs became one of the sparks along with slavery and secession that helped start the Civil War. The Confederate Constitution explicitly banned their national government from imposing external tariffs. The end of the Civil War resolved the tariff issue resolutely and the nation's manufacturing base grew rapidly with ample domestic and foreign investment and a large, protected domestic market. The Federal Government's main source of revenue would be tariffs until the ratification of the 18th amendment authorizing the federal income tax in 1913. Tariffs would not disappear though. Even as the world's largest economy, the US kept high tariffs which culminated in the 1930 Smoot-Hawley tariff meant to help American industries struggling with declining demand due to the Depression. Smoot-Hawley had a large impact on American trading partners, especially the nations of Europe recovering from World War I and Germany in particular who needed to earn foreign exchange to pay reparations debts. However, how much the tariff was to blame for the deepening of the Depression is an object of controversy amongst economic historians though they are in general consensus that it did not help the situation.

In the post World War II world, Smoot-Hawley became representative of the worst protectionist trade tendencies amongst most Western countries. Tariffs were still around though and were used by countries such as France, West Germany, Japan, and the rising Asian economies to recover the industries of their bombed out countries. As America ran a trade deficit with these nations (although it still retained a trade surplus overall until 1971), the global dollar standard, backed by gold under the Bretton Woods agreement, meant that these countries could redeem the dollars they earned from exporting to America for gold. This was an issue of tension throughout most of the Cold War though it was typically handled through back channels and side discussions unlike today's open ruptures and disagreements. Echoes of today's complaints about tariffs and defense spending are reminiscent oft those with President John F. Kennedy who admonished French president Charles de Gaulle and West German chancellor Konrad Adenauer about the need for the US to maintain gold reserves while simultaneously spending large amounts to assist in defense from the Warsaw Pact forces. This tension came to a head in 1972 when President Nixon took the US dollar of the gold standard in order to combat the prospect of huge gold outflows due to dual trade and federal budget deficits.

In the post World War II period declining tariffs globally have been a key feature from bilateral agreements such as the US-Chile Free Trade Agreement to free trade/reduced duty zones such as the North American Free Trade Agreement between the US, Canada, and Mexico, the European Union, or Mercosur in South America. With lower tariffs, global trade has grown faster than global GDP creating a more globalized world that has broadly created greater, though uneven, prosperity and increased the availability of quality goods and services.

There have been benefits and costs to the new globalized world that are not often shared equally by countries or socioeconomic strata. In United States and other developed countries global trade has undeniably lowered the price of many agricultural and manufactured goods broadly benefiting consumers and also encouraged foreign investment in the United States that creates employment and new opportunities. However, many of these gains are balanced by a weakened and increasingly automated industrial base that hurts previously well-paid workers, skilled and unskilled, who participated primarily in manufacturing rather than the FIRE (financial, insurance, real estate) and information technology sectors that have proportionally grown in the economy. Similar concerns can be heard even in newly developed countries like South Korea or Taiwan who benefited from offshoring decades ago only to see their own production shifted to low cost countries like China or Vietnam.

It is these negative impacts that have revived the discussions of protectionism in the United States where it had once become an almost taboo topic. The challenges facing the US economy are substantial and likely not amenable to simple solutions but it is undeniable that a substantial number of Americans are in need of a new economic model to maintain prosperity and a reasonable standard of living. It is not the purpose of this book to argue politics or whether or not tariffs are partially the solution to complex knot of national budget deficits and debt, declining corporate investment, increasing productivity not being reflected by stagnant real wages, automation, and an economy that naturally changes and evolves requiring new sets of skills. Like them or not, tariffs are here for at least the short term and many business owners and managers, having primarily lived through an era of declining or non-existent duties, have to deal with them in ways they previously have not.

The focus of the book is the practical considerations of dealing with tariffs from the perspective of importers, customers of suppliers affected by the tariffs, and exporters. Many large companies have a full suite of legal, logistics, and trade compliance personnel to understand these things. Most companies do not and are new to these issues. The main considerations will be raised here but this book does not intend to be exhaustive. This books is not meant to be a step by step guide on customs brokerage, importing, and the myriad other tasks required to move goods across borders. There are other much more comprehensive guides available. If there is ever a doubt, proper counsel such as from a customs broker, legal expert, or even the US Customs or Border Protection are the proper route.

Chapter 2
Tariffs—Who runs this show?

As stated in the last chapter, the original power to enact tariffs and deal with the commerce of foreign nations rested with Congress. Congressmen like Senator Reed Smoot of Utah and Representative Willis Hawley of Oregon, would propose, amend, and pass tariff legislation to be signed by the president, which in the case of Smoot-Hawley was President Herbert Hoover in 1930.

In the post World War II period trade powers were increasingly granted to the Executive branch by Congress in order to aid in the ability of the US to negotiate favorable trade terms. In particular, it allowed for tariffs to be imposed by executive order in situations where national security was seen to be at risk. The Trade Expansion Act of 1962 was passed during the Kennedy administration in order to deal with the increasing clout of a reconstructed Europe that had formed the European Economic Community (EEC), the economic predecessor to the modern European Union free trade area. As discussed earlier, the US was running a trade deficit at the time with many Western European countries while seeing its goods hampered by tariffs.

The Trade Expansion Act accomplished many important changes. First, it empowered the president to appoint a special trade representative to negotiate trade on behalf of the United States. President Kennedy created the Office of the Special Trade Representative in 1963 with one representative based in Washington DC and the other in Geneva, Switzerland. It also gave the president emergency powers to impose tariffs, particularly in its Section 232 which gave the president the power to unilaterally impose tariffs on products whose import volume posed a threat to national security. The Section 232 power was used several times, most recently by President Donald Trump to impose tariffs of 25% and 10% respectively on a variety of steel and aluminum imports from various countries.

The next major piece of legislation was the Trade Act of 1974. By this time, not just European competition but competition from Asia such as Japan was becoming an issue. The biggest accomplishment of this law was giving the President full negotiating power over trade deals with "fast track" authority that allowed the President to negotiate trade deals that Congress must vote up or down on and neither amend nor filibuster. It also made the Special Trade Representative (which changed its name to the United States Trade Representative in 1979) a cabinet level position in the Executive Branch and also gave him or her a responsibility to report to Congress. In the Trade Act, another relevant trade clause, Section 301, was established. Section 301 was provided to allow the Executive branch to examine trade practices from countries that are deemed discriminatory. If found so, it gives the President authorization to put a stop to such practices. Section 301 is at the center of the current trade war between the US and China and is the authorization for the imposition of US tariffs by the President.

Given the last two pieces of legislation, the ability to set trade policy has not solely existed in the Legislative Branch for some time and disputes over who has the proper power to issue long lasting tariffs are beyond the scope of this book. Nevertheless, once a tariff has been decided upon, the official announcement will be published in the Federal Register, along with percentages and enactment dates. The tariff code list is then updated at the US International Trade Commission (USITC) and Tariffs are immediately collected upon import by Customs and Border Patrol (CBP). Tariffs are not always charged at the port of entry. For example, if goods are destined for a free trade zone in the US, they may transit there duty free and not pay tariffs until they are formally imported from the free trade zone by the importer. It is important to reference the right sources of data to understand if a tariff has taken effect and at what rate. No other non-government website or the website of a foreign government can be considered final or accurate until the Federal Register and the USITC have been consulted.

Chapter 3
Dealing with tariffs as an importer

As an importer of product, you are obviously going to be paying the tariff directly for anything you bring in from China or another country hit with duties. However, much of this is simplified since all but the largest organizations typically use a third party customs broker that holds a limited power of attorney to manage their transport and import of goods. This is good since you do not have to concern yourself with the vagaries of dealing directly with Customs and the various port fees and procedures. However, some basic knowledge is necessary to provide your broker for proper importation of goods.

First, the goods must have an assigned country of origin by the exporting supplier. This is usually the export country, but not always, and can change based on value add to the final goods. Country of origin is useful due to specialized tariffs like the 301 tariffs against only China or special free trade agreements like the USMC (formerly NAFTA) free trade agreement between the US, Mexico, and Canada and the US-Chile free trade agreement.

The default trade treatment for countries is the Most Favored Nation (MFN) status or as it is more commonly known now, the permanent normal trade relations (PNTR) status. All countries not subject to free trade or preference agreements tend to fall into this status.

Second, the goods you are importing must be defined according to a Harmonized Tariff System (HTS) code. HTS codes are a series of numbers subdivided by periods that are used internationally to categorize goods for the purpose of statistical information and imposing taxes and duties. A typical HTS code is: **7217.10.40.40**

This HTS code corresponds to wire of iron or non-alloy steel, not plated or coated and whether or not polished, round wire with a diameter less than 1.5 mm and heat treated in coils not weighing for than 2 kilograms. That's a mouthful.

The detail is due to the levels of the tariff code. The first two numbers, 72, are the chapter which refers to a broad type of good. In this case, 72 is Base Metals made of Iron and Steel. This was one of the first groups of products hit by the global Section 232 tariffs in June 2018 that placed 25% duties on steel items as well as 10% duties on aluminum items.

The second two numbers, '17' help form the four digit heading: 7217. This four digit number drills down to the precise type of product, in this case wire of iron or non-alloy steel. Following these are additional two digit subheadings which more specifically define the product separated by periods. The subheading .10 refers to wire that is not plated or coated but may or may not be polished, .40, refers to round wire with a diameter less than 1.5mm and the last .40, usually for statistical purposes only, indicates this wire is heat treated and in coils not weighing more than 2 kilograms. Together these numbers define the HTS code for the product.

As an importer, you are responsible for letting your broker and US Customs know the HTS code of every product you import. While the shipper/supplier can give recommendations and guidance, ultimately you are responsible for the correct classification (per US Customs) and paying any tariffs and duties. If unsure, you can petition for a classification review by US Customs. However, it is not advisable at all to just select the code you think will cost less or have a smaller tariff. Incorrect classification can trigger an audit by US Customs that can result in fines in the thousands or tens of thousands of dollars per infraction. You are especially on thin ice if you change a commonly used HTS code for an import after a tariff is imposed as a way to avoid the tariff.

To determine the duties, you can check the US International Trade Commission's database at https://hts.usitc.gov . By searching or opening the PDF files for each chapter you will see screens like the below. The first two columns have the HTS code numbers, with the last two being the 'suffix' if applicable. Not all items have a suffix and that is ok as long as the first eight numbers are defined. Next is the 'Article Description' describing the good and the Unit of Quantity used to calculate the item quantity being imported (mainly for statistical purposes). The final columns describe the tariff rates. Column 1 is for the standard tariff rates as applied by legislation. The General column is the rate of general import from almost any MFN/PNTR country while the Special column is for special rates such as from a free trade agreement like NAFTA or the US-Chile Free Trade Agreement.

Column 2 is for tariffs for non MFN/PNTR status countries which the United States typically has trade sanctions or poor relations with. As of 2025, the countries handled by column 2 are Russia, Belarus, Cuba, and North Korea (yes, we do about $30k of trade with North Korea each year).

Heading/ Subheading	Stat. Suf- fix	Article Description	Unit of Quantity	Rates of Duty		
				1		2
				General	Special	
7217		Wire of iron or nonalloy steel:				
7217.10		Not plated or coated, whether or not polished:				
		Containing by weight less than 0.25 percent of carbon:				
		Flat wire:				
7217.10.10	00	Of a thickness not exceeding 0.25 mm	kg	Free[4/3/]		25%
7217.10.20	00	Of a thickness exceeding 0.25 mm but not exceeding 1.25 mm	kg	Free[4/3/]		25%
7217.10.30	00	Of a thickness exceeding 1.25 mm	kg	Free[4/3/]		25%
		Round wire:				
7217.10.40		With a diameter of less than 1.5 mm		Free[2/]		25%
		Heat treated:				
	40	In coils weighing not more than 2 kilograms	kg			
	45	Other	kg			
	90	Other	kg			
7217.10.50		With a diameter of 1.5 mm or more		Free[4/3/]		7%
	30	Heat treated	kg			
	90	Other	kg			
7217.10.60	00	Other wire	kg	Free[4/3/]		25%[2/]

This duty is the likely rate you will pay on importation of the goods. The actual amount will be higher due to port fees, etc. but these are standard.

Once you have determined a product's duty rate, you need to calculate the financial impact. Unlike many countries that calculate tariffs on a CIF (cost of good + freight insurance + freight) basis, the US is relatively less expensive and calculates tariffs on the FOB (freight on board) basis which essentially means that the price shipped from the supplier, plus any freight handling charges to the foreign port or airport of disembarking is all that is used to calculate the cost of goods for tariff calculations. This cost is typically known to Customs as the "purchased value".

One important piece of information for importers who traditionally did informal importations of goods, valued at $2,500 or less and do not require a customs bond, is that informal importations are not allowed for goods subject to quotas or tariff duties so even if your shipment is small, the informal importation route is no longer applicable.

Section 232 and 301 tariffs and Chapters 98 & 99

While most of the chapters in the tariff code deal with different classifications of goods, there are two special chapters dedicated to additional tariffs or special duty free treatment. With the passing of the tariffs from 2018 on, the tariff duty rates were often placed in Chapters 99 and were incremental on any tariffs paid in the General column for imports from China (Section 301) or general imports of steel and aluminum (Section 232). These were expanded with the new US Tariffs in early 2025.

This section frequently changes and giving firm guidance on codes can become outdated but an example below will suffice. Tariffs under 8413.70.10 cover centrifugal pumps for making paper and are duty free under the General column in the HTS. However, when imported from China, they fall under Section 301 tariffs which in this case are enumerated under 9903.88.01 and include an added 25% in addition to the general rate (which was 0% before). The newest tariffs implemented on February 1, 2025 and adding an additional 10% on all other duties from China fall under 9903.01.20 for now.

For example, if buying such a pump from China at a purchased value of $10,000, you would list 8413.70.10 and calculated $0 of duties, 9903.88.01 and calculate $2,500 of duties and 9903.01.20 and calculate $1,000 of additional duties for an effective duty rate of 35%.

The section 9903 handles the bulk of the China section 301 tariffs but review the schedule and Federal Register for any changes. Other tariffs are handled in other parts of Chapter 99. For example, the bulk of the Section 232 tariffs on aluminum fall under 9903.85.25. It is important to work with a Customs broker or Trade Compliance specialist to find with tariff headings need to be added in addition to the general tariff so pay these duties and declare goods properly.

Trade Preference Programs

In addition to free trade agreements, the US is a member to some special trade preference programs such as the African Growth and Opportunity Act (AGOA), the Caribbean Basin Initiative (CBI) and the Nepal Trade Preference Program (NTPP). These are temporary programs that allow partner countries to import certain goods at reduced duties or duty free. These are usually goods such as textiles to help these countries develop their economies by exporting to the US market. These can use certain tariff codes in Chapter 98 in additional to general tariff codes. For example, AGOA and the CBI often use 9802.00.80.

Who Classifies Goods?

It is officially the responsibility of the importer of record (read: you) to correctly classify goods on import. Suppliers can tell or recommend a classification for your goods but if this classification is wrong, and especially if it is believed to have been used to avoid duties, the full force of the law and fines will fall on you the importer. The exporter has no explicit or implied liability here. It is also not the responsibility of a customs broker to recommend HTS designations, though some will give recommendations, and if there is an issue the importer, not the customs broker, is still the party at fault. The US Customs has Import Specialists at ports which may give you an oral recommendation of classification but again, this is not a binding ruling and is not valid at all ports. Therefore it is essential that you categorize goods correctly and make sure the supplier lists the proper HTS code on shipping documents and the invoice (all must match). It is best to have a fully documented procedure on how tariff codes are selected in case there are questions in the future. A documented rationale for each tariff code applied to a product is the best practice.

In most cases, if a good is pretty clear cut, it should not be a problem to find the correct HTS code to use for the shipment that most closely approximates the good. Sometimes things can be more vague, however. For example, let's take titanium golf club heads made in a foundry in China. Is the correct HTS code a cast titanium part (HTS code 8108.90.30 .30) or is it golf club parts (HTS code 9506.61.00.00)? In this case you can use golf club parts because the part is unambiguously used to make golf clubs. On the other hand, for the sake of example, if you import a piece of generic cast titanium that you somehow machine or make into a golf club head later it is not a golf club part since it could theoretically be used to make many things. It is not enough to have a purpose for an import, it must be clear in design and function, known as the Essential Character of the good, to survive a possible audit. The section of the US code 19 U.S.C. § 1481 contains full detail on requirements for importers. You must make sure that the good description, prices, weights/dimensions, and other information are accurately submitted to Customs at import and that procedures do not vary for the same good at different ports.

US Customs Rulings and Classification Determinations

Sometimes there is a question, however, that you can't answer about a part. In this case, the ultimate authority is US

Customs and you can contact them to apply for a determination. Before applying for a determination though, it is useful to search prior US Customs rulings in the CROSS online database (http://rulings.cbp.gov). Here you can search by HTS code, description, country of origin etc. to find past rulings on goods similar or identical to your own. These rulings are binding and therefore if a determination has been made for your exact good, it is the guideline you must follow. If a ruling doesn't exist, you can submit a request for a ruling electronically.

Submitting a request for a determination is a detailed process. Just sending a one liner 'is my widget HTS code X" is not advisable. You should supply Customs with all information possible including the information on your company, port of embarkation and receipt, and as much general and technical data as reasonable to allow them to make an accurate decision on how to classify the good, whether it qualifies for a free trade agreement duty, etc. Once a final ruling is received, which can take many weeks, this ruling should accompany your other import documentation on subsequent imports as proof of the correct designation and tariff treatment.

Requests for Tariff Exclusions

Sometimes you may have a vital good that falls under a tariff regime and you want to see if you can obtain relief for that product class. The process for petitioning to receive an exclusion is relatively simple but tracking the process, much less finding a concrete reason for acceptance or rejection of a request, is difficult. In addition, submission periods vary by type of tariff. For Section 232 tariffs against steel, the request for exclusions is open (for now) for submission at any time.

For Section 301 tariffs, however, the exclusion application period is typically 90 days from the commencement of the tariff. This could change though and official information regarding exclusion request deadlines is published in the Federal Register.

Exclusion requests are specific to companies and items and only one item (as defined by HTS code) is permitted per request. The government is now requiring the filling out of an Excel template that allows consistent applications. Typical information are detailed descriptions, use of the material, information on criticality and why an exclusion is necessary (usually due to single/sole source with foreign suppliers or national security priorities) and other pertinent information for the government to reach a decision.

Once filed, the exclusion will be placed on the public docket and open for public comment for a certain period of time (usually 14 days). Responses are informally supposed to be returned in 90 days but can take longer. If the exclusion is granted, the company will have a one year exclusion of paying duties on the product. For 232 tariffs this is retroactive to the date the exclusion request was made available for public comment. For 301 requests, this is retroactive to the start date of the tariffs. However, again many requests for 301 exemptions were due 90 days from tariff implementation. An accepted exclusion allows the applicant to apply for a retroactive refund of duties paid. To obtain a refund, a form called a post-summary correction (PSC) that mentions the granted exclusion number.

If the exclusion is rejected, the government will give a reason. The easiest is the wrong tariff code for the product. Much more difficult are other objections. In either case, the applicant has the right to apply for a new exclusion with the correct HTS codes or to answer the objections listed in the first rejection letter. Some importers have noted that similar products applied for exclusion are accepted and rejected for apparently inconsistent reasoning. However, even in this case the only remedy is to file another exclusion request.

Duty Drawbacks

As an importer, even if you are required to pay tariffs on a product, you have the opportunity to receive up to 99% of the tariff cost back if you destroy or re-export the goods to foreign customers. Duty drawback is the process by which you document the destruction or re-exportation of dutied goods and apply to US Customs for a partial refund on duties paid. Duty drawback is a very complicated and labor intensive process. It also involves extensive, detailed record keeping by the applicant in order to guarantee acceptance. Oftentimes, even large firms will contract with outside logistics, brokerage, or consulting firms to assist in the duty drawback process. The costs in time as well as outside help need to be balanced against the expected dollar value of the drawbacks one can receive. If minimal, a business must make its own choice as to whether the time and effort are worthwhile.

The essence of the duty drawback is to prevent a country's manufacturers or distributors from being penalized when competing in foreign markets. Without drawbacks, a country would essentially shoot its exporters in the foot by increasing their costs due to import tariffs. Not only the United States but many countries with high tariff rates such as Brazil allow duty drawbacks so their firms are sometimes more price competitive in export than with domestic customers. While helpful, it is important to note that drawbacks do not allow companies to avoid paying tariffs at import, even if they know the import will belong to an exported order. The exception can be free trade zones where the goods can be parked without clearance as long as they are re-exported from the free trade zone and not formally brought into the US. Tariffs must be paid, the goods tracked, and then drawbacks applied for on export.

Drawbacks can typically take several months or even longer to be paid. Another key point is that in almost all cases, duty drawbacks are unavailable for re-exports to nations with which the United States has free trade agreements. So if you import a good from China, add it to a product and re-export to Mexico, Canada, or Chile, the duty drawbacks are not available. This was true under NAFTA and will likely remain true under the new US-Mexico-Canada (USMC) trade agreement and is true under the US-Chile FTA. The government also reserves the right to deny duty drawbacks in some special tariff situations. The most prominent current example is the Section 232 tariffs implemented in 2018 against global imports of steel and aluminum. The decision was to not allow drawbacks for these tariffs though the drawbacks are available for Section 301 import tariffs against Chinese goods.

Drawbacks fall into two broad classes. The first is for goods that are re-exported as parts of larger assemblies or just re-exported. The second is for goods that are destroyed before use or re-sale. The first case is far more common and will be discussed first. Drawbacks for imported goods that are subsequently re-exported fall into a few classes.

The first class is the traditional manufacturing duty drawback where goods are imported from a foreign country, tariffs are paid, and the goods are subsequently a value add in a new product that is re-exported. For a manufacturing drawback, the goods must be transformed and they have to be re-exported within a five year time frame of import. After export, the exporter has three years to apply for duty drawbacks with US Customs and must maintain records for three years after the drawback is processed. Up to 99% of tariffs can be refunded but this is fully at the government's discretion.

A second case is called substitution drawback. In substitution drawback a company imports products that it pays tariffs on, but also buys the same product, in both function and quality, from domestic companies or foreign companies in countries with a free trade arrangement with the US. These products, all the same but from different sources, are made into a larger assembly that is then re-exported. Depending on the quantity of exports, an exporter can apply for duty drawback on the imported duties parts as if all the exported products had imported parts, even if they don't. They theory is that the multiple sources of supply are completely interchangeable and if the imported duties goods can be "substituted" the exports can be treated the same. Of course you can only receive up to 99% of tariffs paid on duties parts in the drawback. Unlike the manufacturing drawback, however, you must re-export substituted imported products within three years of importation.

Another common case is the same-condition/unused product duty drawback. This is essentially for products that are imported, tariffs paid, and then re-exported in the same form without being used in the United States. This is common for re-sellers, distributors, or spare parts orders. The parts must be re-exported within three years of importation and the duty drawback must be filed within three years of exportation. However, as will be explained later, unlike the previous drawback examples advance notice is required for Customs before exports in these cases.

The second class, relatively newer and rarely used, is the drawback provision for destruction of imported goods. You can receive drawbacks for destruction of imported goods that tariffs have been paid for if it is done in three years and also done under the supervision of US Customs. According to the US Customs website:

You must have proof of the export or destruction, as well as proof that duty was originally paid. A bill of sale or airway bill is valid proof of export and a CBP Officer must witness the destruction of the goods. Without proof of export or the destruction, the claim is not substantiated.

There are many other minor and specialized types of drawbacks specific to certain industries that can be used if they apply but the ones just described make up the majority of all duty drawback claims.

The Duty Drawback Process

Applying for duty drawback is not as simple as filling out a form after exporting goods. Substantial prep work is required before beginning the drawback process. First, one must submit the correct forms to US Customs to detail the import, manufacture, and export details. Second, one must sometimes post a drawback bond, especially if you are eligible accelerated payment of drawbacks owed. In filling out the various documentation forms, often professional assistance is helpful if not essential. One should contact your customs broker or a reputable trade law firm or consulting firm to process the paperwork if this is your first time or if you are looking for large sums for reimbursement. Remember, tariffs and drawbacks are like taxes—it is not always logical and requires knowledge and experience.

Customs Forms

The typical Customs forms involved are CBP 7551 and CBP 7552 which are the basic information on imports and subsequent products covered by the drawback and the details of internal manufacturing and intercompany transfer respectively. CBP 7553 is used for the advanced notice needed for same-condition, destruction of goods, and other drawback actions that require advance notice to Customs.

The forms constantly change and it is essential to read the accompanying instructions and supply all necessary details on the goods and the process of changing them (if applicable). Everything that you enter on these forms must be backed up by internal documentation before the forms are submitted. This internal documentation can be reviewed by US Customs at their request and cannot be conjured post-hoc to meet the requirements of a Customs audit or one risks heavy penalties, even in excess of the drawback amount received.

Drawback Bonds

An exporter can apply to the CBP for accelerated drawback payments which substantially shortens the amount of time between filing and payment. This requires among other things, a detailed application process (again best done with professional help to maximize chances of being successful), a forecasted amount of drawback that will be accumulated over the next twelve month period, and importantly a drawback bond.

Importers typically always have bonds with CBP in order to cover possible shortfalls in Customs fees or tariff payments on the importation of goods. Drawback bonds are a bit different and are secured to cover the CBP in case the accelerated drawback payments are in error and need to be reversed. The minimum amount of the drawback bond is the forecasted drawbacks to be received in the next calendar year.

Documentation

In line with the drawback process, one needs to maintain careful records of all imported products used in drawback, their transformation, intercompany transfer, and eventual export. Along with typical documents such as invoices from suppliers, import documentation, and purchase orders from customers, products that are transformed must be clearly matched to assemblies in bills of materials, etc. and production records must be transparently maintained. In an audit, CBP should be clearly able to trace a product from import to your factory or warehouse, to manufacturing/shipment of another location, and finally export.

In addition to product part numbers or SKUs, it is a good idea to record manufacturing information such as lots, expiration dates, heat numbers, etc. Again, this information must be in hand before the application and maintained for three years after drawback has been received just like you keep your old tax documents in case the IRS wants to audit.

Duty drawbacks can lift a huge weight off the shoulders of a company affected by tariffs that has many export customers. At minimum it is financial relief. Even better it allows one to compete against foreign competition not hobbled by similar import duties from foreign suppliers. However, it is not a simple process and requires intense internal record keep as well as organization to support the application and possible audits. Given the required work as well as the cost in personnel time and likely outside help, it is important to evaluate the expected financial benefits from a drawback. If export orders are occasional and small, it may not be worth the time and effort. This can only be decided by the exporter after weighing the costs and benefits.

Also, in seeking professional help, be sure to review several sources and review costs under your detailed scenario you provide them. Costs should be transparent and free of hidden fees. Also, beware of firms that "guarantee" drawback success. The rules at CBP are constantly changing as well as the conditions for drawback as Section 232 shows. In addition, ask the firm to provide proof of insurance and make sure their terms only reasonably limit their liability in case there are damages to you due to their negligence or incompetence. Some firms draft these terms in ways that leave them with no liability so your own legal review is usually necessary. Most firms will try to limit liability to fees paid though depending on your agreement you can negotiate a higher amount covered by their insurance. It depends on the firm and there are no hard rules but no liability is not acceptable. Finally, ask for several references with similar operations to call on to gauge how they have performed in the past.

Chapter 4

Dealing with tariffs as a customer of an importer

Most of the preceding chapters have covered the situation with you as the importer where you pay the tariffs due directly on import. These situations, though complicated at times, are pretty straightforward overall. If you are a customer of a supplier who is an importer, however, you may be hit by price increases or shortages of products due to tariffs you may not understand or be able to control. This chapter covers these situations.

Price Increases

Almost all companies in the US received price increases during 2018 citing "tariffs" as the cause for the price increase. These are usually honest and legitimate though sometimes companies will leverage these to get relief for their margins if they think they can. Unless you have a strong relationship (or extreme leverage) over a supplier, you will be paying some of this. It's no one's fault, just life. Unless the supplier switches their source of supply, which can also raise costs, there is no way around this.

How much should you pay though? Obviously, you should pay no more than the tariff amount, but beyond this it can get complicated. There are relationships where both sides split the expense 50/50 30/70 etc. However, there are also situations where you should not be paying the full amount. In short, unless you are being sold an imported product that is nearly unaltered and retains the country of origin (i.e. Made in China) you should not pay full tariff cost. Let me explain.

Tariffs are applied to the material portion of the good that is imported. For example, a supplier imports a part from China at a 25% Section 301 tariff. This part is then 25% of the material cost of the final assembly. Therefore the price increase on the material cost of the good is 0.25 x 0.25 = 0.0625 or 6.25% of the assembly cost. Note I underlined the word "material" to emphasize this is only one part of the cost. All manufactured parts have a labor component as well. Assume this assembly is 50% by cost labor and 50% by cost material. The final price increase is then the material percentage times 6.25% or 0.5 x 0.0625 = 0.03125 or 3.125%. This is a price increase for sure, but far from a full 25% hit. This assembly likely is "Made in the U.S.A." as well due to the majority of value add being domestic.

On the other hand, if you are buying a private labeled widget from China from a distributor, the 25% is pretty close to exact, but still you can argue that a 25% price increase overpays the tariff. The reason is this 25% is on both the part cost (imported) and their markup. So the part cost and markup are both being inflated by 25%. Theoretically you should only pay 25% times (1 – the product's gross margin). So if they are making 10% gross margin on the part, you should only owe 0.25 x 0.9 = 0.225 or 22.5%. Under this calculation they would receive the same amount of profit, though their gross margin will decrease due to the higher cost of the product from the tariff. The key issue however is this calculation requires a supplier essentially disclosing their markup which they are extremely reluctant to do for good reason. In this case, negotiation may get you a couple percentage points off which can always help.

One of the most difficult tariff related price increases to deal with is the indirect price increase caused by tariff where domestic manufacturers raise their prices since they now are less exposed to the cheaper foreign imports. This causes a general price shift in the entire marketplace and often price volatility as we have seen in 2018 in US steel and aluminum markets. When faced with a general market price increase the best strategy is to track materials as closely as possible and make sure the increases you are seeing are in line with the market. There are multiple sources for this data online, and unfortunately they are not always cheap. For scrap, American Metal Market (AMM) is a typical industry standard while multiple platforms from companies like Argus Media and Thomson Reuters offer current and historical base metal pricing .

A final note is that if a supplier is proposing you pay the full brunt of the tariff, the product must have a foreign country of origin the supplier can confirm. If it is called "Made in the U.S.A." there is value add in material or labor that should dilute the tariff expense.

Drawbacks as a non-importer

It may come as a surprise that if a supplier's product has foreign content that they paid tariff on, you as the customer can receive the drawback. However, this requires coordination with your supplier and both you and your supplier cannot receive the drawback; only one or the other. Basically, the importer/supplier must submit a certificate of delivery (CBP form 7552) to you which will assign you the right to drawback. If the importer is buying custom or specialized equipment for your use only, it is also good if they note your company and your PO# on their purchase order to the foreign supplier for traceability purposes. Once the certificate of delivery is in hand, with the appropriate record keeping per the previous chapter, you can apply for a duty drawback.

Tariffs magnify material and currency related increases

One final negative aspect of tariffs from a cost perspective is that they magnify underlying increases in product cost due to material increases or currency fluctuations. For example an x% increase in product cost due to a material related price increase at the (foreign) supplier translates into a (1+x) times tariff increase. So a 5% material cost increase from a foreign supplier coupled with a 25% tariff gives a full increase of 1.05 x 1.25 = 1.3125 or a 31.25% increase. This is obviously 1.25% more than just adding the 5% and 25% together. Similar calculations apply if you are buying a product in a foreign currency that fluctuates against the US dollar.

Conclusion

The international trade environment has never been easy and the recent uncertainty caused by the rise in protectionism globally will not make it any easier. However, financial considerations aside, tariffs are just like any other tax or regulation to comply with. Clear and organized records, transparency, and obtaining the right help if necessary can make it navigable and allow your firm to still compete well in the domestic and global marketplace.